# The Informed Real Estate Investor

A Step by Step Guide to Becoming Rich in Real Estate

Patrick G. Esposito

ALL RIGHTS RESERVED. No part of this publication may be reproduced or transmitted in any manner whatsoever without written permission from the publisher.

© 2009 by Patrick G. Esposito

This publication is designed to provide accurate and authoritative information in regard to the subject matter covered. It is sold with the understanding that neither the author nor the publisher is rendering legal, accounting, or other professional service. If legal advice or other expert assistance is required, the services of a competent professional person should be sought.

In many ways, this book has been years in the making, through my various experiences in real estate. There are many people who I have learned from in different ways. A big thank you goes out to all of them. In particular, this book is dedicated to my family. I first learned about real estate from my father, and his insight has been instrumental throughout my career. My mother has also always been there for support. My brother Don was the person who gave me the idea to write this book, and my brother Fred's suggestions have been helpful also. I first met my fiancée Beth when the real estate market was at its peak. Her perpetual support has been most appreciated and very helpful.

# Introduction

You have probably heard the phrase "If only I knew then, what I know now." This book is designed to give you the information you need to know, and not spend the next ten years trying to learn on your own. Real estate has been a great wealth builder for many years, for many people. When the economy is good, you can make money in real estate; when the economy is bad, you can make money in real estate. The most important asset to have when attempting to make money in real estate is knowledge. You can and will learn on your own. Try to learn as much as you can from other's experiences also.

To be most effective, this book is best used as a tool in your investing arsenal. Feel free to underline, and make notes where need be. Refer back to this book as you need to. You may even want to bring it with you when you inspect the houses. Although, this book discusses many aspects of real estate investing, there is much more information out there. Don't let your quest for knowledge stop here. Let this be a starting point. If you are an experienced real estate investor, let this be part of your continual search for knowledge. Real estate can be a wonderful way to make money, prepare for a secure retirement, or just keep up with inflation and live a comfortable lifestyle. This book is meant to build a strong foundation, and therefore discusses a lot of basic real estate information. One needs this basic information no matter what level of investing that you are currently at. This book is meant to teach, motivate, and inspire. It is the sincere intent of the author that you will achieve all of your real estate dreams.

Never give up, never stop learning,

Pat Esposito

# The Informed Real Estate Investor

*An informed real estate investor has a decided advantage over another investor.*

## Table of contents:

1. Set Goal, Be Realistic, and Write it down.......... 7
2. Determine What Area You Will Work in……….. 10
3. Materials That Will be Needed........................14
4. What to Look For...................................... 17
5. Finding the Good Deals............................. 19
6. Assessing the Neighborhood........................ 30
7. How to determine market value..................... 33
8. How to inspect a property........................... 39
9. How to qualify a property..........................64
10. Making a purchase offer ........................... 70
11. Turn your real estate contract into an option.... 74
12. How to make everything negotiable..............78
13. After the seller accepts your offer................81
14. Re-negotiating price concessions................. 84
15. Assigning the contract............................. 90
16. Getting Started Before You Get Started.......... 93
17. Choosing a Contractor............................ 95
18. Purchasing to Hold as a Rental................... 99
19. 21 Mistakes Beginners Make ....................105

It has been said that more money has been made from real estate investing than all other businesses combined. When most people are ready to retire, their biggest asset is usually their home. Real estate is all around us, and if you are willing to work hard, you can probably find a good deal about once a week, and a great deal at least once a month, and a super deal about 1-2 times a year. After you are finished reading this book, you will know where to concentrate your efforts. That is one of the keys to success, especially in real estate. You must know where to look for the good deals, and constantly be searching.

# Chapter 1

## Set Goal, Be Realistic, and Write it Down

Before you start any endeavor, you must have a goal. Maybe your goal is just to learn about real estate investing, and put together one deal your first year. That is a great goal to start out with. Maybe your goal is to be another Donald Trump, and purchase many properties. That is a great goal also. That second goal will take longer than the first, so it is probably not realistic to say you will do many, 10 or more deals your first year. It may happen, but you should start with goals that are so realistic, you can not possibly fail. Some people set goals that are too high, and they never reach them.

If you have some experience, then your goals may be different. With experience behind you, it is very realistic to do one or more deals a month. You can realistically become a millionaire investing in real estate, but it will probably not happen your first year. The key to setting and achieving goals is to believe you will achieve that goal. Write down the goal, read the goal every day, and believe you will achieve it. Set some sub goals, and try to experience some success each day. It also helps to have a plan of action. When you are finished reading this book, you will be prepared to formulate a plan, and put it into action. That plan will involve one or more of the various ways to find good deals, how to qualify those properties, and how to submit purchase offers.

Most people start investing in real estate part time, and over the years you can become very wealthy, even on a part time basis. It is not recommended to start investing in real estate full time without experience. By the way, there are many ways to purchase real estate, which may or may not involve you using your own money. Sometimes you may not even take title to a property and only control it and still make money. If this is the case, you are still considered a real estate investor. You are investing your time, and maybe your money. You can also be called a real estate consultant, real estate professional, or real estate entrepreneur. Whatever you choose is up to you.

Sometimes a beginner is so anxious to get started and set the world on fire, that they do not prepare properly, and burn out in less than 60 days. Abraham Lincoln said that if he had 10 hrs to chop down a tree, he would spend the first 5 hours sharpening his ax. So it is very important to prepare, and to learn. Now on the other hand, some people attend seminars, read all of the real estate books, and never do anything. Remember to set your goals, and write them down. For example:

Each week I will look at two houses, and submit at least 4 offers per month.

Then, at the end of each week, you can see if you have reached your goal (of course you will reach it).

<u>There is power in goal setting.</u> When you set a goal, you start to release the power of creative vision. You have to envision the dream, before you make it a reality. Goal setting is the first important step toward turning your objectives into reality. When you set the goal, do it in a positive state of mind, and believe that you will achieve your goal.

*People with clear written goals achieve more than those without goals.*

The first important step toward achieving your goal is to put it in writing. When it is written down, the goal becomes real; you gain that little extra push that is important starting off. Make your goals measurable and specific. The clearer and more specific you make your goals, the better able you are to envision it. The better the vision, the closer you are to achieving it. Don't just say, "I want to make a lot of money investing in real estate." That is not a goal; that is a wish. A goal would be more like the following:

In 6 months from today, which will be (write that date down), I will make $10,000 from investing in real estate. I will purchase a house, and flip that house, and make $10,000.

The more you look at your goal, the more power, and motivation it gives to you. Start today and you are well on your way to achieving your goals.

> *"The will to win means nothing, without the will to prepare."*
>
> *- Juma Ikangaa*

# Chapter 2

## Determine What Area You Will Work In

Determining what area that you will look for properties in will be instrumental to your success. There are different factors to consider:

A. What is the proximity of this area to where I currently live?
B. What is this neighborhood like? Would I want to invest here, or work here, and feel comfortable driving around, and walking in this neighborhood?
C. Am I already familiar with this neighborhood?
D. Is this an up and coming area?
E. Are there any restrictions in this area, as far as rentals, or construction?
F. Is this an area that is convenient to shopping, churches, and schools?
G. Is this in a flood zone?
H. What is the area zoned for?

I. Is this a high crime area?

These are some things to consider. Eventually, you will determine for yourself, what area you would like to invest in. You will also learn from other investors what areas are popular for investors. The three top rules to consider when purchasing real estate is location, location, location. You can invest thousands into a house, remodel the kitchen and bathroom, and paint the interior and exterior. These things can certainly increase the value of a property. After you own a property, you can not change the location. Therefore, location is the number one consideration when considering purchasing a property. The more you know about a property, the better position you are in to make a wise investment decision. A good rule of thumb is that you should not purchase a property that you would not feel comfortable walking down the street at night. Research the area, and try to learn as much as you can about the area. If there is an abundance of homes for sale in a concentrated area, find out why.

When looking at property values, circumstances can change from block to block. There is no substitute for experience. Drive around the neighborhood, frequent the local merchants, and talk with the neighbors. Sometimes you can find some real eye openers, good or bad. As time goes on, you will become an expert in your area. Another advantage to concentrating on certain areas is that if your investments are confined to certain areas, this will make your management job easier. If you are spread out with your investments, you will not be able to have a handle on things as best as you should.

You may find a great looking house with much potential, but if the area is not sound, walk away. If you have any misgivings about a particular neighborhood, others will also. Don't buy a house because it is a great house, with big rooms, and would look great fixed up. Buy because it is in a good, if not great, neighborhood, and the house is solid also. You can improve a house with carpet and paint, amongst others things, but you can't change the neighborhood.

Another good rule of thumb is to invest only in properties that are within 45 minutes of where you live. You will be devoting much time and effort into this property, and of course getting to know the neighborhood. The closer to home, the more convenient it will be for you. There are probably hundreds of wonderful investment properties within 20 minutes of where you live. Always keep in mind; there is opportunity all around you.

*Three top rules for real estate investing: Location, location, location.*

"The successful warrior is the man with laser-like focus." – Bruce Lee


"If you chase two rabbits, one will escape."
- Anonymous

"The first and the best victory is to conquer self."
- Plato

When shopping for a house, remember: location, location, location.

# Chapter 3

## Materials That Will Be Needed

There are certain things you will need to run this business. The following are the tools of the trade.

    A. Legal pad
    B. Pen
    C. Flash light
    D. Tape measure
    E. Camera
    F. Answering machine or voice mail
    G. Fax machine
    H. Contracts
    I. Business cards
    J. Calculator
    K. Map
    L. Telephone

These are some of the things that you will need to help you prepare for your imminent success. When you purchase the tools of the trade that you will need, you will be investing in your business, and your future. You can also write these off on your tax returns as business expenses. Consult with your accountant and save your receipts.

Today's world of real estate investing is much different than just 15 years ago. The computer has changed things drastically for the better. You can sit at your computer and get comparables, even look at the comparables right on the computer. Real estate investing of yesteryear had us going to each house to check it out. Drive through the neighborhood, and get to know the area. We still need to do that on the legitimate prospects. Sitting at your computer, you can look at fifty houses, and decide that only ten meet your criteria to look at. You have all the information right at your fingertips, to evaluate the best prospects. You do not need a computer to invest in real estate, but it certainly helps.

If you are serious about making this a business, even just part time, you will need business cards. A lot of business is done through networking, and you certainly want to look professional. If someone has a great deal to tell you about, you certainly don't want them to try to remember your name, and figure out how to get in touch with you. On your business cards, you want to have your name and phone number. You don't necessarily need your address, but it will not hurt. You may list a fax number if you have one, and an email address. You can state that you are a real estate investor, and maybe print what type of properties you invest in.

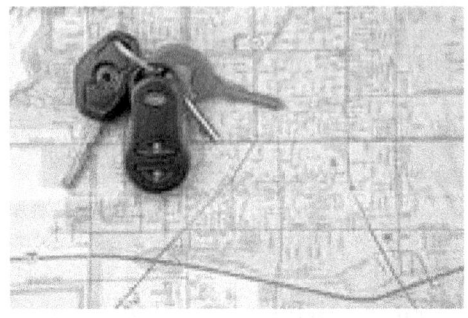

A map is a vital tool in your arsenal for success

Remember to bring the camera.

# Chapter 4

## What to Look For

Many books have been written about all of the different types of real estate to invest in. They range from residential, to commercial, to raw land. The best starting point is the simplest. Single family houses make a great investment if purchased correctly. There are a number of reasons for this. They are easier to find comparables for, and they are best for starting out, when learning how to qualify a property. When selling a property, they also seem to have the largest market. You can resell this property to a homeowner, or to an investor. They make great rentals, or you can put someone in there on a lease-purchase. This is also the biggest market to find properties. If you only concentrate on locating single family homes, you can become wealthy. As you get better at this, though, you will find other types of deals. Duplexes, triplexes, and up also make great investments. Raw land at the right price could be a good investment.

It is good to concentrate on a certain segment of the market, but to be familiar with other segments also, for there will be deals out there that will present itself to you. Even if there is a good deal that you are not interested in, if you are able to assess the feasibility of this property, you may be able to assign this to another investor.

The best scenario is to find the worst house in the best neighborhood. After you have chosen an area you are comfortable investing in, then you want to find a house that is under market value. As you start to look at more and more properties, you will get a good idea of the market values in a given area. We will discuss this in more detail later on. You want to find a distressed seller, or a property that is in need of repair.

As a general rule, especially when first starting out, stay away from conversions. In other words, don't buy a one family house and convert it into a two or three family house. Sometimes this can be profitable, but usually this type of scenario has its share of headaches. You may have to go before the zoning board, and code enforcement, and upgrade the electric, plumbing, etc. Keep it simple, there are many good deals out there.

*"Obstacles are what you see when you take your eyes off your goals." – E Joseph Crossma*

# Chapter 5

# Finding the Good Deals

There are many ways to find good deals. Some of the best ways are quite simple. Remember, though, that the key to success in anything is persistence, and perseverance. The best way to start looking for good deals is right in your local newspaper. Look for properties that are for sale in the area that you have chosen to work in. Also look in the price range that is ideal for an investment. The best market is usually middle class, or slightly lower, or slightly higher. If you work in the high end market, those types of houses do not usually make good rentals. And if you work in the lower end, those properties may be difficult to sell, and are not the best neighborhoods to work in.

You can find out a lot about a property or an area just by reading the newspaper. The next step of course is to call and ask about the property. Always be prepared with a pen and paper. Some questions to ask would be:

A. Where is the property located?
B. What type of construction is the building?
C. What is the area zoned for?

D. How many bedrooms and baths are there?
E. Is there a basement or attic?
F. Is there a garage or a shed?
G. How many units does the building consist of?
H. If it is more than one unit, are the utilities separate, and who pays, the landlord or the tenant?
I. What type of flooring is inside?
J. How old is the roof?
K. What is the property size?
L. What is the square footage of the house?
M. What are the annual property taxes?
N. What condition is the house in?

Some ads in the paper will be houses that are listed with a real estate agent. These are good ads to call on because you can learn a lot from a real estate agent, and they will have other houses to show you. That is the next best place to find good deals, through a good real estate agent. Try to find an agent who is familiar with investment property. If you find a good real estate agent who understands what you are looking for it can be very profitable. There are a number of good reasons why you want to have a real estate agent as part of your success team. Experienced real estate agents generally have a lot of education and experience. One of the keys to success is to use other peoples experience, and other peoples education.

Agents are also good at negotiating. They are good to have as a buffer between you and the seller. They are knowledgeable about the neighborhood, and can help guide you with regards to pricing whether it be when submitting an offer or listing a property. They are usually on the cutting edge when it comes to market information. They can help you obtain valuable information you need when it comes to active, pending, and closed sales. They can give you valuable information such as how many days a property has been on the market, or how many bedrooms or bathrooms may be in a particular house. Agents are always networking, and sometimes an agent may find out about a house before it hits the general market. Real estate agents have access to the multiple listing service (MLS). This service has a world of information on properties that are currently active on the market, pending, or sold. This is all valuable information you will come to appreciate. A good real estate agent has capable negotiating skills, which will come in handy when submitting your offer.

A good real estate agent is vital to your success.

There are good agents, and not so good agents. Find an agent who has experience dealing with the type of properties you are interested in. They should also be familiar with the neighborhood you are looking in. A real estate agent is one part of your team. The other people you will come to rely on will be an accountant, an attorney, a contractor/handyman, a plumber, an electrician, an insurance rep, a banker/mortgage rep. You may find yourself with more than one person in any of these positions. We call this your success team, although your team members may never meet one another. If you are just starting out, you can bridge the gap of inexperience through the association of your success team.

Other ways to find good deals may include dealing directly with a builder or developer. Sometimes when they overbuild they are looking to move properties at cost, and these are new houses or condos. Also, as you drive around the neighborhood, look for properties that may have code violations, tall grass, boarded up windows. These are signs of a distressed seller. Look for properties that are for sale by owner. Sometimes you can get a better deal than if a property was listed with a real estate agent. Look for properties that may have management problems. Talk with people, ask around the neighborhood. Bank foreclosure/REO properties are always a good source for good deals. The banks do not want to be in the real estate business. You may pick up some real bargains.

Here are some tips on buying REO/foreclosures. Do your homework, as much as you can. Try to find out about the history of the property? Why did the former owners lose this house to foreclosure? Did someone die in the house? Does it have a mold problem? Like a good detective, always ask questions. Determine accurate market value, presently, and when it is repaired. Ask how many other offers are being presented on this property. Submit a <u>preapproval</u> letter with your offer. Do not confuse this with a <u>prequalification</u> letter. Don't ask for repairs to be done, or have an inspection done up front. After your offer is accepted, then you can have a contractor inspect the property, and you can use his estimate to help lower the price. If there are other offers on the table, offer to split the fees with the bank, such as the title insurance, and the transfer fees.

Be sure to give your business card to everyone.

Let everyone know who you are, and what you do.


Another really great way to locate good deals is to network. Let people know what you do, and what you are looking for. Sometimes you can even offer to pay a finders fee. You can network through your friends, and family. You can also network with people you work with, or see at church, or other social functions. It is also very beneficial to join, or attend a real estate investment club. This is networking at its highest level in this business, when you are discussing business and possibly doing some deals with like minded individuals. An association with an organization such as this could prove to be invaluable.

Another way to find deals is to drive around the neighborhood. Look for properties where the grass needs to be cut, or the shrubbery is overgrown. Sometimes these properties are abandoned. If you can find out who pays the taxes, and get in touch with the owner, you may land a really good deal. Look for realtor signs or even (FSBO) for sale by owner signs. Don't be afraid to hand out your business card or a flyer to people when driving through the neighborhood. The deals are out there. The key is to look where the properties are advertised, such as the newspaper, or the MLS . The second key is to let everyone know what you do and what you are looking for.

Many times, For Sale by Owners are motivated sellers.

Many good deals can be found in the local real estate section.

## Who is a motivated seller?  - A motivated seller is someone who wants and needs to sell a property ASAP.  Many times the motivation is so high that they are willing to take a loss.  The reasons for selling a property can be numerous.  It is always in your best interest to find out the sellers reason for selling, and determine their interest level.  The following is a partial list of motivated sellers:

1. Behind on payments, or in foreclosure - No one wants to lose their house to foreclosure. It lowers their credit score, is embarrassing, and may take many years to recover from. The lender may also try to get a deficiency judgment against them.

2. Divorce – When a divorce happens, many times one person is not in a position to keep the house. They need to sell, and are thinking more emotionally than rationally.

3. Illness or death – Unfortunately, there are times when things happen, sometimes unexpected, and certain moves must be made. A house may need to be sold to settle an estate, or just to pay some bills.

4. Frustrated real estate investor – Not all real estate investors are walking around with piles of cash and big smiles. Whether it is management problems, cash flow problems, or liquidity, you can sometimes find the motivation level high amongst this esteemed group.

5. Upside down, short sale – When a real estate market depreciates, a seller may find the value of a property less than the mortgage amount. Sometimes it can get so out of balance, it makes sense to sell on a short sale. A short sale is when the lender is willing to take less than the mortgage amount to settle the debt.

Always be on the lookout for motivated sellers. This is the key to making money in real estate. There is an old real estate saying: "You make money when you buy, you realize it when you sell". Buy right; spend your time tracking down the motivated sellers.

This is a distressed seller, could you tell?

*"I am not discouraged, because every wrong attempt discarded is another step forward."*
*– Thomas A. Edison*


*"A man's doubts and fears are his worst enemies."*
*-William Wrigley Jr.*

*"I do not think there is any other quality so essential to success of any kind as the quality of perseverance. It overcomes almost everything, even nature."*

*- John D. Rockefeller*

# Chapter 6

## Assessing the Neighborhood

One of the keys to success in real estate investing is knowing how to qualify a property. With experience, and the right kind of training, you will become proficient at this. On a very simple level, the steps to qualifying a property are to determine the market value or potential market value after repairs, and the cost of repairs. Once you have determined this information, you can determine what price should be paid for the property.

On a deeper level there are other things to consider. After you start to get experience, you will start to get a hunch, or an intuitive feeling for a good deal. Remember the three most important things to a good deal: location, location, location. In other words, the location of a particular property will be extremely important in determining if this would be a worthwhile investment. The ideal location would be a house in a middle class to upper middle class neighborhood subdivision where all of the houses are basically the same market value more or less.

When you are looking at a property, assess the neighborhood. Ask yourself these questions:

A. Is this a good neighborhood, where just about everyone is gainfully employed?
B. Is this a high crime neighborhood?
C. Is this a drug neighborhood?
D. Where is the nearest church?
E. What type of denomination is the church?
F. How far is the closet grocery store?
G. How far is the closest gas station?
H. How far is the closet grammar school, and high school?
I. Are the other houses on the block well maintained?
J. Do the neighbors next door have dogs, and if so, what kind?
K. What is the percentage of homeowners and renters?
L. Is this in a flood zone? (Remember, this will require flood insurance).
M. Stand in front of the house, and look up the block, and look down the block. Is this the type of neighborhood, you would want to live in and raise your family in?
N. Is this the type of neighborhood, you would not want to live in, but you think would make a great rental?
O. How far is this from public transportation?
P. What kind of rent would this property command?
Q. How does this property compare to the other properties on the block?
R. Is there anything very nearby that would detract from the property, such as a junk yard, a train, a city dump, a kennel, a bar, a gas station, etc?
S. How close is public transportation?

Is there an overabundance of houses for sale in the area, if so why?

# Chapter 7

## How to Determine Market Value

The key to determining market value is to do your homework and find out what similar houses in close proximity are selling for. The more information that you can get about similar houses in the area, the better you will be able to determine accurate market value. The best way is to find similar properties right on the same block. If they are not on the same block, try to get them as close as possible, at least in the same neighborhood. You will need to find houses that are similar in square footage, construction, bedrooms, baths, garage, and age. Those are the main things.

Other things to consider are the condition of the property and the location. Does the house have additional features, such as a laundry room, fireplace, or pool? You will want to obtain at least three comparables. Compare the comparables one at a time to the subject property. Compare a 3 bedroom, 2 bath house to a 3 bedroom, 2 bath houses. If all you can find is a 3 bedroom 1 bath house, then you would adjust that by adding 3,000- 5,000 to the value of the subject property. When determining accurate market value, you will need to use properties that have sold as comparables. If you can only find properties that are still for sale, they can give you an indication, but it is not as strong as a property that has actually sold.

When looking for properties that have sold, your real estate agent should be able to give you this information. As you gain more experience, your ability to determine a ball park market value will become better. This ability will become invaluable when you call on properties over the phone and ask questions to decide whether to view this property or not. When you are able to ask the appropriate questions over the phone, and already know something about the area, this will help to save you much time. You may call over the phone on say 25 properties, and decide to look at 10 of them. Out of that 10, you may find 2-3 that qualify as a good deal. In a given month, you may look at 40 properties as apposed to trying to look at 100. You may not be able to look at 100, and out of the ones that you were not able to look at, there may have been a good deal.

Initially, you will want to look at as many houses as possible. This is how you will learn. Later on, you will be able to prequalify houses, and will be able to save much time just by speaking over the phone. If you are an experienced investor, you may already be at this point. *Remember, knowledge is a tool, and the more you use this tool, the more effective it becomes.*

When you are driving through a neighborhood, even if you are not looking at a specific house, call on some of the houses that are listed for sale. There may be a good deal there, and you will build on your storehouse of knowledge. When another property becomes available in that area, you will already have market knowledge. You will be able to make a quicker and more accurate decision. Constantly try to learn as much as you can about the areas that you want to invest in.

Remember to read the real estate section of the newspapers. Sunday is a great day for this. Besides the <u>houses for sale section,</u> there are pages and pages of stories, and articles, and letters about real estate. Many times there are articles about specific neighborhoods or subdivisions. You can also learn about different laws or rules that may or may not affect you. It may not affect you now, but it may in the future.

3 keys to learning market value:

A. real estate agent
B. drive through neighborhood, call on signs
C. read newspaper, especially Sunday real estate section.

*"You can tell what a man is by what he does when he hasn't anything to do."*     *- Anonymous*

*"We are what we repeatedly do. Excellence then, is not an act, but a habit."*
*- Aristotle*

*"Formal education will make you a living. Self-education will make you a fortune."*
*– Jim Rohn*

*"He, who acquires knowledge but does not practice it, is like one who ploughs a field but does not sow it."      - Anonymous*

If you persist, you will succeed, you are well on your way.

# Chapter 8

## How to Inspect a Property

Unless you are a contractor or handyman, you may not be familiar with the repair costs of a house. Of course, the more houses that you look at, the better you will get at this. When looking at a property, ask questions. Ask questions of the real estate agent, and write questions down. Later you can call contractors on the phone and ask questions.

It is important to inspect the property as thorough as possible. This section will provide for you a good foundation on which to develop your skills. Your inspection should be thorough and comprehensive, covering all aspects of the grounds, exterior and interior structures, systems and appliances. It is extremely important for you to take your time when inspecting a property in disrepair. Remember to take notes. Remember, although it is important to be as accurate as possible, final estimates should be left to an experienced contractor. Initially, you are attempting to determine only a "ballpark" renovation cost in order to determine a realistic purchase offer amount.

It is important to realize that estimating the exact cost of property repairs or renovations is almost impossible. However, reasonably accurate repair cost estimates are critical in determining the profit potential of a distressed property. Your prime objective in the initial stages is to approximate the general cost of required repairs to enable you to submit a reasonable and intelligent purchase offer. Remember....This is a preliminary procedure. Do not become consumed with preparing exact repair costs until the seller's motivation level has been assessed, and a purchase offer has been accepted. Leave all final estimates to an experienced contractor.

You can use this section as a reference guide for estimating repairs that are needed. Remember, experience is always the best teacher. The more time and effort you spend looking at properties requiring repair, the more qualified and competent you become at estimating repair costs.

## Evaluating the Grounds

Your first step is to evaluate the grounds of the property. Start your property inspection on the outside of the property and work your way to the inside. Keep an eye out for areas that are potential problems, and any features that may enhance the property's marketability.

# Landscaping

Check for tree branches that overhang a roof. Overhanging tree branches can damage the roofing material, and prevent the roof underneath from drying. Dead trees can endanger the home itself and neighboring properties. A termite nest in any dead tree could indicate potential infestation in the house. Trees too close to the foundation have the potential for damaging the foundation wall or causing water seepage into the basement. On the positive side, a treed lot can provide shade and privacy while muffling traffic noise.

Check any fencing on the property. Fencing in good repair provides some level of privacy and security. It also outlines and separates the property from neighboring homes. Look at the lawn. Does it need to be reseeded or new sod installed? How about the shrubbery around the property? Does it need to be trimmed, or do some shrubs need to be replaced?

## Patio/Deck

A patio or deck will generally enhance the value of a property. In addition to providing additional functionality and entertainment potential, it appears to add a good deal of room to a house. When inspecting a patio, ensure it is pitched for proper drainage. Also check for any cracks or heaving. A patio of permanent construction may prove to be more durable than one of bricks or blocks layed over a sand base. Decks should generally be constructed of pressure treated lumber. Check for signs of rotting or warping. If a painted deck is blistering and peeling, it may need to be stripped, primed and repainted.

## Pool

A pool can be an attractive feature to certain buyers, but it generally detracts from the marketability of a property. Potential buyers, especially those with children, often shy away from a property with a pool because of the potential for accidents and liability problems. When inspecting a pool, check the liner for wear and tear, and the foundation for visible signs of stress or cracking. Be careful to evaluate any factors which may increase liability. The pool area should be fenced and well lit. Check for ground fault interrupter outlets in the pool area and the condition of the plumbing and filter. Repairing pool damage can be costly. Be cautious.

## Driveway

If the driveway is either concrete or blacktop, check for cracks or erosion along the sides. If the driveway is badly cracked or eroded, some sections may need repairs or replacement. If the entire driveway has to be replaced, the cost could be thousands of dollars. If the driveway is crushed stone or gravel, see if it is rutted, washed away or has standing water. If so, the driveway may re-quire additional stone or gravel.

## Evaluating the Exterior

## Foundation

One of the most important things to examine when inspecting a house is the foundation. The age of the house will generally determine if the foundation is rubble-constructed, concrete block, poured concrete, or brick. It may even be a mixture of the above if an addition has been built onto the house. Check the foundation for general deterioration that allows moisture or water to enter the basement. This could require expensive repairs. If the foundation has a large separation, there may be serious structural damage. If so, an engineer should inspect the property to assess the foundation's integrity.

## Roofing

The best time to inspect a roof's condition is after a rainfall. Walk around the house and examine the roof covering, taking note of the pitch or slope. A roof with a good pitch or slope is less likely to leak than a flat roof with roll roof covering. Check the flashing around chimney and stack vents. Look for general signs of aging, or if the ridge of the roof is sagging. Look for patched or damaged sections, or different colored shingles to find repaired areas. Determine if the roof has more than one layer of shingles. If not, repairs may be limited to putting a new roof over the old. If two layers of shingles exist, and both are in poor condition, it is likely that both layers must be completely removed and replaced with a new roof. The process is significantly more costly than just putting a new roof over the old.

## Wood Exterior

The wood exterior on a property generally consists of windows, trim, doors, and door frames. Examine the exterior to determine if scraping, puttying, or painting is needed. Check for rot or any signs of deterioration at the bottom of doors and door jambs. Open and close doors to see if they fit snugly without sticking. Check window housings, sills and sashes for signs of rotting. Determine how much of the wood exterior requires repair, replacement, caulking, paint or stain.

## Exterior Walls and Siding

The exterior of a house has many forms of siding including brick, stucco, aluminum, vinyl wood, asbestos, etc.

<u>Brick</u> - When inspecting an exterior brick wall, check for cracks in the bricks. Also, check the wall for bulges. This could indicate the mortar has failed. Check the pointing of the brickwork to see if it is intact, loose, crumbling or wet.

<u>Stucco</u> - Many older homes have stucco exterior walls. When conducting your inspection, look closely for cracks in the stucco. This can be a sign of water entry. Look for bulges, an indication that the stucco has pulled away from the framing. If the bulge is small, the problem is not likely to be severe. However, if an entire wall has bulged, the foundation may be suffering from differential settlement. This condition requires closer examination by a trained professional.

Aluminum, Steel, Vinyl Siding – All forms of siding have advantages and disadvantages. Whatever the form, the current siding should not be replaced unless it is in excessively poor condition. Determine that all siding is secured snugly to the side of the house. Loose siding may indicate that the wall behind the siding is damaged, or that the nails used to secure it have come loose or fallen out. Also, see if the siding is level. If not, this may indicate a problem with the exterior wall under the siding or a settlement problem. Attempt to determine if the siding was used to cover up a cracked or deteriorating exterior wall.

Wood Siding – A large number of homes have what is called beveled clapboard siding. Usually this type of siding is painted. Examine the condition of the existing paint, and determine if scraping, puttying, and painting is required. Stand at each corner of the property to see if the siding is level, or has any bulges or waves along the exterior walls. Check for pieces of damaged or rotted wood. This may be a sign of water migration behind the siding or insect infestation.

Asbestos Shingle Siding – Make certain the general condition of the siding is good and free of loose or missing shingles. Determine if the siding needs repainting. Cracked, broken, or missing shingles require replacement. Since asbestos is a known carcinogen, shingles must be removed by a certified asbestos removal company. This can be a costly process.

Porches – The porch is the area most vulnerable to decay and insect infestation. It is important to examine a porch closely to determine if it can be repaired. Use a screwdriver to check the railings, balusters and porch posts for rot. Poke at the base of posts, or wherever two members join and/or water might settle. Test the floor for sturdiness by jumping on it. Examine the condition of the floorboards for obvious visible signs of poor maintenance. Closely examine any wood members in direct contact with the soil. If the porch is in a generally deteriorated condition, it needs to be completely rebuilt or removed. Replacement or removal of a porch can be quite expensive.

Garage – Inspect the general condition of the structure and make certain that it is relatively free of any major cracks or settlement problems. Examine the condition of the concrete slab floor and determine its general condition. Look up at the roof rafters for evidence of water entering through the roof covering. Use a screwdriver and probe for rotted or damaged wood. This could indicate water damage or insect infestation. Check the condition of the garage door and how well it opens and closes. If the garage has an electrically operated door opener, make certain it operates properly.

# Evaluating the Interior

## Windows

Check all windows for a snug fit, and examine the sashes and sills for decay. Also check to see if the windows open and close properly. Determine which windows need repair, and which ones need replacement.

## Carpeting

Determine the general condition of any and all carpeting in the house. Many times a carpet can be cleaned to look almost new. Where carpeting needs replacement, pick up the carpeting; determine if the floor is plywood or hardwood. If the floor is plywood, carpet replacement is necessary. Hardwood floors do not always require new carpeting because they may be refinished.

## Hardwood Floors

Examine the general condition of the hardwood floors. Areas in poor condition, that are aesthetically unappealing, or have uneven floor boards will require complete refinishing. Areas with superficial surface stains or water marks can easily be restored through light sanding and one application of polyurethane.

## Pet/Urine Odors

The problem of pet/urine odor should be taken very seriously. Pet/urine odor can be almost impossible to eliminate completely. All carpeting must be removed and may even require the sanding and refinishing of the flooring beneath the carpeting.

A coat of paint can dramatically change the appearance of a house, inside and out.

## Walls and Ceilings

If they have not recently been renovated, older homes will have plaster walls and ceilings. If a home is fairly new, the walls and ceilings are drywall construction. Examine all plaster walls and ceilings thoroughly for damage. Minimal damage can be repaired very simply by taping and spackling. If the damage is extensive, complete removal and replacement of the area may be required. Tap several areas to ensure that the plaster walls are firmly set, and that no deterioration is apparent. Examine the areas all around doors and window frames. Check for water stains which may indicate leaks from the exterior. If the walls are papered, several layers may be present. Often, wallpaper has been applied to plaster walls to hide imperfections. As a rule, all wallpaper needs to be removed and the walls prepared for a fresh coat of paint.

When inspecting a house with drywall construction, check for any exposed nail heads. Also note any exposed tape where drywall sections are joined. These may be signs of settling, excessive vibration or moisture in the studs. Such sections can generally be patched with joint compound wherever they are damaged or loose.

If walls are paneled, check to see if the paneling is firmly nailed or glued in place or if there are any bulges. Examine the ceiling for any signs of water stains. Such stains indicate leakage from the roof, gutters or exterior walls. They may also be caused by leakage from a bathroom or kitchen on the floor above.

## Bedrooms

The number, design and layout of the bedrooms, as well as how they function and flow throughout the house, play a key role in influencing homebuyers. If bedrooms are too small or without adequate closet space, this can be considered a major drawback to a house. This problem adversely affects the market value and marketability of the property. Many older homes suffer from this shortcoming.

## Kitchens

Depending on its condition, the kitchen can either greatly add to or detract from property marketability. Be sure to check the walls, floors, and ceiling for cracks or water stains. Check countertops for signs of wear, burns or stains. Inspect the sink for cracks, chips, and stains. Check cabinets to see if they require minor refinishing, repainting, or replacement. If a kitchen is old and obsolete, you may have to modernize the entire kitchen to enhance property marketability. Plumbing and electrical work should also be inspected. Check the condition of floors. Should they be replaced with ceramic, or vinyl?

Check underneath the sink for potential leaks.

## Bathrooms

Check that the bathrooms are adequately sized. Look for cracks or stains on the walls, ceilings or floors. Make sure the fixtures are tightly installed and sealed. Inspect the tiles, grouting and caulking around the shower or bath. Plumbing and electrical work should be inspected. Turn on the faucet and look underneath the sink for leaks. Flush the toilet, check that it flushes properly. An out of date bathroom should be modernized to enhance property marketability. Renovations of kitchens and bathrooms generally provide the best return on your investment dollar.

## Attic

Notice if there is a full size attic or a crawl space. A full sized attic may be finished or unfinished. With an unfinished attic, check for appropriate insulation, usually 6-12 inches. Inspect for water damage or signs of leakage. This could indicate the need for roof repairs, especially if the evidence is clearly recent. If the attic is finished, check the type and adequacy of heating and air conditioning for the area.

## Basement

The basement is the most important area of the house to inspect. Most visible signs of structural or system problems will reveal themselves in the unfinished portion of the basement. Check exposed foundation walls for cracks, bulges, or separation. Look for signs of seepage or dampness. A musty odor usually indicates moisture coming through cracks or the foundation material. Visible water stains on foundation walls may be evidence of prior flooding problems. If a sump pump is present, test for proper operation. Exposed floor boards from the level above may show signs of insect infestation. Poke a screwdriver into sections of the floor boards or sill plate. If the screwdriver penetrates these areas, or if the wood appears to be generally soft, this is a clear indication of rot or insect infestation. If the basement is finished with sheetrock or paneling, be sure to check at the base for flaking or water stains. Dropped ceiling panels may also exhibit signs of water damage.

Always check the basement, sometimes you may find surprises.

If you are handy, you may wish to do some of the repairs yourself.

# Evaluating the Systems

## Plumbing

It is not uncommon to find a combination of galvanized piping, brass piping and copper tubing when inspecting an older house, especially if it has been modernized. Old, obsolete forms of plumbing may require complete replacement in order to comply with the newer more stringent code standards.

Water pressure is the first thing to check when inspecting the plumbing system. Check several faucets and all showers for adequate water flow. A lack of water pressure may indicate a supply problem or leaks in the supply pipes. While inspecting the pressure, check for proper drainage and note the condition of pipes below the sink.

Check for any leaks or rust requiring repair or pipe replacement. If the main drain line is visible in the basement, look for signs of deterioration or leakage. Drain lines may be made of galvanized, cast-iron or plastic piping. Inspect for leaks, signs of corrosion or sections that have been replaced. Take notice of any hint of sewage smell in the house. This usually indicates damaged or deteriorated vent pipe. If a house has been vacant for a lengthy time period, and the plumbing system has not been adequately winterized, or the water has not been drained from the entire system, you can anticipate damage from frozen water lines. Carefully inspect all plumbing for burst pipes.

## Electrical

Very often, in older houses, the electrical system must be updated. These houses usually have 110 volt, 30-60 amp system, which is inadequate to accommodate today's appliances. This service is housed in a fuse box instead of a circuit breaker panel box. To determine electrical capacity, count the number of outlets and switches installed throughout the house. It is not uncommon to find only 1-2 outlets per room, although one per wall is ideal.

Very often, the electrical current is carried through obsolete knob and tube wiring. This type of wiring is extremely thin, with sections held together by ceramic knobs. When this type of wiring is present, anticipate the need for complete rewiring. Generally, you are required to upgrade to a minimum of 100 amps and install a circuit breaker panel box with a main shutoff breaker.

If a panel box is present, check to see if circuits are overloaded with an excessive number of outlets or fixtures. Appliances such as air conditioners, washing machines, dryers and refrigerators should each have separate outlets. Examine electrical wiring wherever possible. Sections of exposed wiring can be located in the attic or basement.

Wiring should also be checked at wall receptacles or fixtures. Any deteriorated or damaged wiring will need to be replaced.

Count the number of outlets in each room. The general rule of thumb is that a minimum of one outlet should be located in each wall. Kitchens and bathrooms should be equipped with ground fault interrupter (GFI) type outlets. These rooms also require a larger number of outlets to accommodate the use of several appliances. If extensive renovation is anticipated in an older home, local code enforcement may require the electrical system be completely upgraded to meet new safety standards. The decision to upgrade may be determined by the municipality's electrical code enforcement inspector.

# Heating

Determining the type of system and what type of fuel is being used for heating is important. The heating system is one of the most expensive systems to replace in a house. Heat is conveyed by steam, hot water, or forced hot air. The boiler is fired by gas, oil, or electricity.

## Steam/Hot Water Heat

Look for water stains, water on the floor, broken gauge glass and signs of extensive corrosion on the outer cover of the boiler. If the floor shows stains or signs of water, this could indicate a leak or a crack in the internal section of the boiler. This damage may require that the boiler be replaced. Look for maintenance tags attached to the boiler to determine the last date serviced and the types of repairs completed. Examine the condition of the cement connecting the flue pipe to the chimney wall. Look for large cracks or broken pieces of cement. If the house is occupied, turn on the boiler ( by using the wall mounted thermostat) to determine if the boiler is functioning.

## Oil Fired Systems

When checking oil fired systems, determine if the oil burner gun is old or new. Make sure the heat exchanger is not cracked or broken. The air flow across the heat exchanger should be uniform with the flame centered.

## Gas Fired Systems

For your safety, leave this inspection to an expert.

If the volume of air is not uniform, a section of the heat exchanger may fail. If the furnace is not functioning properly and if there is a low volume of air over a section of the heat exchanger, the temperature in the heat exchanger wall will build up and cause it to fail. Look again at the combustion section and see if flames from the burner are heating the bottom of the heat exchanger. These flames should be centered in each section of the heat exchanger. If they are not centered, a section of the heat exchanger may be overheating.

## Electrical Heat Systems

If the heating system that you are inspecting is an electrically fired forced air system, the heat will be produced as soon as someone adjusts the heating thermostat. When inspecting an electrical forced-air system, determine where the furnace is located in the house. The furnace should be centrally located in the house so that the ducts which supply heat throughout the house can be as short as possible. Shorter ducts will reduce heat loss in the house.

Regardless of the type of system used, or how the system is fired, it is important to measure the level of efficiency and consistency of the heating system's performance. Whenever possible, allow the heating system to run not less than ten to fifteen minutes to provide adequate time to monitor the system's performance on a room by room basis.

Carefully examine the general condition of radiators or baseboard heating elements located throughout the house.

## Central Air Conditioning

A central air conditioning system uses a forced hot air heating system's ducting. An air conditioning unit consists of a compressor, condenser coil and evaporator coil. The condenser (located outside the house) is the component that disperses the heat removed from the living area. When inspecting this component, look for signs of rust or deterioration. Be sure it is securely mounted to an adequate base. Always turn the system on to determine how well it functions.

## Sewer/Septic

A septic tank is used to collect and dispose of sewage in a house not served by a city or town sewer system. A septic tank system is composed of a tank, pipes and a drainage field. If the septic tank has not been properly maintained, it could require extensive repair or replacement. Whenever possible, determine the tank capacity and the date it was last cleaned. Replacement of a septic system is very expensive. A permit and a formal inspection by the township is usually required. In certain areas, the city code enforcement requires architectural plans to be prepared and submitted to city officials for approval.

## Well

If a house is not served by city or town water, a well with a water pump delivers water from the ground to the house. The system should be thoroughly checked for functionality, with an emphasis on water pressure. If the system does not provide adequate water pressure, it usually indicates the need for service or replacement. If the well is old, a new one may need to be drilled. As a rule, it is wise to test well water to determine if it is suitable for human consumption.

## Evaluating the appliances

Make it a point to turn on every appliance that is expected to remain with the property. Determine the approximate age and condition, as well as how well the unit functions. Check if colors and styles coordinate.

Turn the stove on to determine if all the burners and oven function properly. Examine the interior of the refrigerator and freezer for cleanliness and functionality. Old, non-functioning or poorly maintained appliances usually require replacement.

This property is in a great neighborhood, and makes for an ideal investment

This house may be small, but a 2 bedroom house with a shed still makes for a nice rental.

# Chapter 9

## How to Qualify a Property

After you have determined the market value of a property, and/or the market value after the property is repaired, and determined the cost of repairs, then you can work the numbers to see if this is a feasible deal. The objective is to have 40% equity in a property before repairs. The amount of the repairs should be no more than 10% of the appraised value. For example, if a house would appraise for $100,000.00 after repairs, an investor would pay no more than $60,000.00 for this house, sometimes as much as $70,000 depending on the location. The repairs should amount to no more than $10,000.00. The profit potential will be more on properties that require an extensive amount of work.

  Remember, at this point it is important that you have done your homework, and are working with accurate numbers. Also keep in mind what your objective is with this property. You can assign the contract, usually your primary objective. You may want to keep this one, fix it and resell it, or fix it and keep it. In either case, you want a property that will be attractive to a homeowner, or an investor.

You want to stay away from the following:

A.   **Heavily fire damaged properties** - Any time there is fire damage, there will be more damage than the eye can see. If it is heavily fire damaged, it is not worth the effort.

B.         **Major foundation problems** – These problems may be able to be fixed, but is it worth it? You would need to contact a contractor, and possibly an engineer. You would probably need to get a permit to fix the problem. If you are a novice, stay away from major foundation problems. If you are an experienced investor, proceed with caution.

C.         **Sinkholes** – Hire a contractor, and an engineer to determine the extent of the damage. Better yet, stay far away.

D.         **Major termite damage** – Many houses have termite damage, and a pest control company can rectify this. Major termite damage means that there is also major damage to the house. Many times this will mean structural damage. The house is only as good as the structure.

E.         **Drug neighborhoods** – Neighborhoods that have drug problems attract those people as tenants, and scare away the good ones. Properties in these neighborhoods are only potential problems.

F.         **High crime neighborhoods** - High crime neighborhoods and drug neighborhoods go hand in hand. You will find houses at what appear to be great prices, but these are not good investment properties. Purchase a property where you do not have to be afraid to walk down the block.

G.         **The neighbors on either side have dogs such as a pit bull or a Doberman** - If there are menacing dogs on either side, or in the rear of the house, you will have a hard time renting or selling this property. You can certainly put up a big fence, but it is usually best just to walk away from this one.

This may have much potential, but stay away from major renovation work.

What to look for in a good deal:

    A. Good location, safe neighborhood, near churches, shopping, and schools. In certain areas, it helps if there is public transportation.

    B. Repairs that are needed are mostly cosmetic.

C. Taxes are relatively low, or at least reasonable.

D. House has a functional layout, with a nice size yard that will attract a nice family.

E. The house in is an area with mostly homeowners, as opposed to a mostly rental area.

F. There is adequate parking; a garage certainly is a plus.

    After you have inspected a property and worked the numbers, and have determined this is a good deal, then you would need to submit an offer to the seller. After the seller accepts your offer, this is when the real fun starts. The seller may accept your offer, or the seller may counter your offer with another price. Remember, this is a business, and not to take anything personal. The seller may not look at it from this point of view. They may be upset or insulted by your offer. The objective here is to make a deal, but only if the numbers are right.

If the seller accepts your offer, move ahead to the next step, which is to put your package together to offer for assignment to a prospective buyer. If the seller counters your offer, then take another long hard look at your numbers. If your intent is to assign this property, then you may still be able to make a deal. A $10,000 assignment fee is great, but a $2,000 assignment fee is better than nothing at all.

When properties are appreciating, you will build equity.

When the housing market is depreciating, it is a great time to buy from a distressed seller.

At the right price, this house looked like it had potential. Although a nice cash flowing duplex with the proper tenants for many years, when the market weakened, this property became hard to sell

# Chapter 10

## Making a Purchase Offer

After determining repair costs, and market value in repaired condition, then you are prepared to determine an offer amount. You want to offer an amount that will yield a profit after the repairs are made. We will assume at this point that you will attempt to assign the contract. If you choose to keep the property for yourself, then there will be more profit for you. You want to have a formula to determine an offer amount. Without the correct information, everything is just a guess. Here is a suggested formula:

Market value (after repairs) minus repair costs x 60 %= offer amount. Depending on the location, and condition, sometimes you can go as high as 70%. But especially when assigning a contract, it is better to stay closer to 60%. The better deal that you have, the easier it will be to assign the contract.

When you write up an offer, you may use a realtor's standard contract to submit your offer. When you write in your name as the buyer, right after that you want to write <u>and/or assigns.</u> There should also be a clause in the contract that you need to check off stating that you may assign this contract. Let the seller know that you may assign this contract. Try to get 10-14 days to accomplish this, before you have to back out.

Always try to put down as little as possible in the way of a good faith deposit. Try to put down $10.00 to write up the contract. The most you should leave on deposit would be $100. After you find someone to assign the contract to, then that person would put up the additional down payment to be put in escrow until the closing.

After you submit the offer, and you have agreed on a price, the next step is to have a contractor inspect the property, to confirm your estimated repair costs. This is done for a number of reasons. It is much better to move ahead with accurate numbers. It is also easier to assign a contract with a contractor's estimate. If the estimate comes in higher than expected, this is an ideal opportunity to renegotiate the contract.

Now put your paperwork together. The following is what you will need:

A. Property Information Form
B. Market Study Analysis
C. Signed Contract
D. Property Inspection Report
E. Pictures
F. Contractors estimate (helpful, but not necessary). After the seller accepts your offer, you will then definitely need this.

Real estate investing is all about making deals.

A good real estate agent is an important member of your success team.

# Chapter 11

## Turn Your Real Estate Contract Into an Option

One of the best strategies for making short-term profits with real estate is to buy a less than perfect house (one that needs cosmetic repairs) from an anxious seller, clean it up and resell it.

To help guarantee your profits, it's a smart idea to combine this "what to buy" strategy with the financing strategy of an option.

*Strategy: Reduce your risk and your cash outlay by using an option to purchase.*

Let's say you are about to buy a house that you intend to fix up and sell. You're concerned that you might not be able to resell the property prior to the time required for you to buy it. An alternative to buying the house outright is to sign a six-month option to buy the house. With the option you pay the owner for the right to buy the property within the specified time period. Options reduce risk. The payment to the seller, called option consideration, is also less than a down payment. But how do you turn the original discussion with the seller from a purchase to an option?

From the negotiating point of view, there are two main items that you need to agree on – time and legal format.

Before you buy, a careful inspection should reveal all problem areas, but it doesn't always happen that way. An option gives you time to negotiate further after you start your clean-up if you discover additional items in need of repair. Also, you will not have as much out-of-pocket cash on the table initially. And by delaying the close, you might be able to avoid many of the usual closing costs. If you find a buyer for the property before the option expires, you can have the new buyer pay the closing costs rather than you. In effect, you sell your option to the new buyer.

The difficulty in delaying the close depends on your previous conversations with the seller. If you originally agreed to buy as soon as an agreement is reached, you will have more work than if you started out talking about a delayed close. If the idea of a delay is new, try to get all items in agreement and settled first. Once there are no other points of contention, let the bomb drop. "There is only one small problem remaining". When you say that, most sellers get knots in their stomachs. "It is not the price or the terms." Now anything you say will sound like good news. "We will need to close a little later than I had originally expected."

*Strategy: Rather than introducing an option agreement, use a local real estate contract and convert it to an option.*

The second needed change is agreement on a change of legal format. It is not difficult to turn the real estate purchase agreement into a unilateral contract instead of a bilateral agreement. This means, rather than an agreement to buy and sell, you have an agreement allowing you to buy at will, and the seller must sell.

*Strategy: Negotiate for the right to back out of the option.*

Offer the early and immediate release of all or part of the earnest money deposit should you decide not to buy the house, or if you assign the contract to someone else. If the seller doesn't agree, you could back out altogether using the escape clause "Subject to the approval of my partner". Since you should never release that clause until the last minute, you can use that to make the buy/sell contract an option.

Here's how you would negotiate with the seller.
You might say "Since we have everything in order except my partners approval, I can go ahead and give you part of the earnest money deposit to hold in return for the extension of the closing date."

This way you have kept the *subject to* clause intact, made your extension seem more favorable and with release of part (or all) of the earnest money you have given option consideration.

Once verbal agreement is reached on all this, it is time to write it up. Here is what you need. Add to the contract that:

A. The sum of X dollars, or the earnest money, is to be released to the seller as option consideration.
B. Time of closing will be chosen by the buyer, anytime in the future but within the next six months.
C. In the event the buyer fails to close within six months, the buyer must give the seller an additional X dollars to extend the time of closing up to three more months or forfeit the option/earnest money.
D. In the event the closing is not done in a timely manner, the loss of the earnest money by the buyer to the seller will be the only remedy available to the seller, and this contract shall be null and void and of no further force or effect.

The last four statements will turn any real estate purchase contract into an option. It also would be best to add:

E. In the event this contract does close, all option/earnest money paid to seller will apply toward purchase.

Options are simple, powerful and highly profitable in the hands of smart investors.

# Chapter 12

## How to Make Everything Negotiable

You are a negotiator – we all are. In real estate investing there are specific negotiating strategies that will make you thousands of dollars if they are applied properly.

*Make your initial telephone contact with the seller positive.*

The telephone call is usually your first contact with the seller. It is the first time the seller is getting to know you. As you are talking, the seller can "hear" a lot about you. For example, he can tell whether you are friendly or businesslike, a beginner or a pro.

It is important that you decide what impression you want to present to the seller. Your strategy as a new investor would be to "smile" when you are speaking on the telephone, be honest and listen to the seller carefully. People will try to "mirror" back to you the image that they are getting of you. If you are open and honest, then they will tend to be open and honest, too. How people respond to you is even more important than what they actually say.

*Gather the key facts in a friendly, non-threatening manner.*

By asking the right questions, you can gather all of the information needed to conduct a successful negotiation in five minutes or less. Most people are afraid to ask personal questions like, "What is the principal balance left on your mortgage?", "How did you arrive at your asking price?" or "Are you able to receive some of your equity in the form of a monthly cash flow?" Don't be afraid to ask, and remember that fact finding is the key to all negotiations.

*Remember to take notes as you are speaking with the seller.*

The asking price and the offering price are your starting point for all real estate negotiations. At times the seller will not give you the asking price for the property, and may suggest that you make an offer. Don't! What may seem like a low-ball offer to you may seem like a great deal to them.

Ask the seller what the asking price is and then make an offer verbally or in writing. Eventually it will have to be a written offer for it to be legally binding.

*Always flinch at the asking price.*

When the seller gives you the asking price, no matter what that price is, your strategy will be to verbally flinch by repeating their figure in a loud questioning voice, as if it is much too high. You will find that at this point many sellers will either lower their asking price immediately or they will begin to justify why they feel this is a fair price for their property. Once you know the seller's asking price and you have made an offer, you have the basis of the negotiation.

*Always create a win-win deal.*

With all truly successful negotiations, both parties must feel that they have gotten what they need and want. When you gather the information by asking questions, you will know exactly what the seller needs and wants for this to be a win-win deal. A seller may not be able to put into words the reasons he or she needs or wants to sell the property. At this time you want to emphasize the positives of this deal for them, such as a quick closing, buying as-is, etc. Keep in mind the sellers may want to get out of a deal later on if they can't justify it to themselves or others. Help the sellers see how and why it is a winning deal for them.

*Offer less so you have negotiating room.*

To pad your offer, offer less than what you would really pay for the property and ask for more personal property than you really want. If you've ever made an initial offer that was accepted without any hesitation by the seller, you probably offered too much. There is an old saying that you can always go up in price, but you can never come down. Actually, you want to submit an offer that will encourage the seller to at least counter your offer. If the seller does not counter your offer, walk away. If your first offer is accepted, you can ask for a lower price and justify it after having a home inspection performed. The most important thing to remember is to always be fair and honest, make it a win-win deal, and be open to creativity.

Always make it a win-win deal.

# Chapter 13

# After the Seller accepts your offer

After the seller accepts your offer, and you have this in the form of a signed contract or purchase offer, you need to have a contractor inspect the property. You can call a professional property inspector, which may run anywhere from $100-400. A more conservative approach is to have a contractor, or handyman inspect the property. If you are attempting to assign this contract, this written estimate will certainly help, although the investor may want to have an independent inspection done.

*Should you renegotiate the purchase amount?*

Once you have all of your accurate information, then you will be able to determine what a fair offer for this property is. Your first offer that was accepted may be a great deal. If after you receive an estimate from your contractor, and you determine that the offer is too high, then you may need to renegotiate. At this point, you have some advantages. Once the seller accepted your offer, he started to anticipate a closing. His mind was focused and intent on selling this property to you. You both shared the common objective of getting the transaction to the closing table.

Another advantage is having a written contractor's estimate. This may show needed repairs that even the seller was not aware of or the extent of the needed repairs. At this point, the seller knows he has a ready, willing and able buyer he is dealing with. Even if you are not the end user in the transaction, he knows that you have investors that you work with and have access to. If he decides to back out of this transaction, he will have to start all over looking for another investor.

The more intelligently and responsibly you conduct yourself during the renegotiating process, the more effective you will be in securing a better purchase price. The specific circumstances associated with your transaction determine the type of communication that best suits your objective.

After you purchase the house, will you look to rent it, or sell it?

Whatever you do, you will make this into a moneymaker.

# Chapter 14

## Re-Negotiating Price Concessions

Price concessions often make the difference between purchasing the property or withdrawing the purchase offer. At this stage, the seller does not want you to withdraw. It is not uncommon to receive concessions of $20,000 or more. Obtaining a price concession converts a marginal opportunity into a very profitable one.

Sometimes you can renegotiate verbally, other times a written letter may be needed. Although it will take some time to understand when and how to strategically apply these techniques and letters, you must understand that every investment opportunity is always open to renegotiation. Renegotiation of contracts is common when purchasing distressed real estate; because there is often much more renovation needed than initially meets the untrained eye. Without getting an adequate price concession, often the deal will prove to be a losing proposition. You should not renegotiate a purchase price when the deal is extremely profitable, and renegotiating would risk the seller's withdrawing from the transaction.

    Once you have a written contractor's estimate, go back to the seller and request a more favorable purchase price. Explain that the property requires significantly more repairs than you initially anticipated. If the seller is emotionally attached to the property, the written estimate may help him see what a realistic selling price should be.

Don't be afraid to ask for a lower price.

Negotiation tips:

a. Never get emotionally involved – Once you start to fall in love with a property, you will do your best to acquire it. You will see all the good things about the property, and dismiss the bad. Remember, it is all about the money, and there are many deals out there.

b. Never be the first person to name a figure – When someone says "Make me an offer", they are fishing for your bottom line and motivation. Let the other person give their asking price before you name an offer amount.

c. He who talks first loses. When you are negotiating and you give a verbal offer, or ask for something else in the deal, ask the question, then remain quiet. If you speak, you lose some of the leverage you just had.

d. When selling a property, ask for more than you expect to get, when offering to buy a property, offer less than you are willing to spend.

e. Don't act too interested. Be sincere, and of course ask questions. If a seller senses that you have a strong interest, he is more likely to hold closer to his asking price. If he senses that you have a weak interest, he may lower his price to raise your interest level.

f. When negotiating, remain upbeat, positive, and friendly. People like to do deals with people they like. Be likeable. Even when you submit a low offer, don't be insulting. You can even let the seller know beforehand it will be a low offer, and why.

g. Try to create a win-win outcome. Everyone wants to feel like they made a good deal. Even if you just made the greatest deal of the century, let the other party feel like a winner also.

h. Put yourself in the other fellow's shoes. It can give you a perspective that may help in the long run.

i. Focus on the issues, not personalities. Sometimes negotiations can become tense. You may start to dislike your opponent. Once this happens, take a step back, review the issues, and remember, this is what it's all about.

j. Don't blame, point fingers, or call names. Remember, people will give a good deal to people they like. Don't always let the other party know what you are thinking, especially if it is adversarial about them.

k. Ask questions to find the other person's needs and wants. The more you know about the other person, the better position you are in to try to make it a win-win. Maybe they can do a little better on the price if they can rent the house for three months.

l. Do your homework. Prepare yourself as best you could, before starting the negotiating process. Know about the market value, and the repair costs, and reason seller needs to sell.

m.  Don't negotiate against yourself. After you submit an offer, it is the sellers turn to accept, counter, or reject. If the seller asks you to do better, ask first for a counter offer. If he refuses, walk away. If you raise your offer without the seller first giving you a counter, then you are bidding against yourself.

n.  Get it in writing. When you and the other fellow agree on something, get it in writing. We are all busy with things on our minds, so it is easy to forget. Make a habit of taking good notes.

o.  Make sure that the person you are dealing with is the decision maker. You may use this tactic for your purposes sometimes, by needing to go to a higher authority for approval.

p.  Be a good listener. It is important for communication. You can learn much from someone else who likes to talk.

q.  Know what you are negotiating for. This comes back to doing your homework, and working your numbers. This also lets you know how flexible you can be to make a deal.

r.  Have a back up plan. Be prepared to walk the walk or walk out. Sometimes there are different ways to create a win-win. Be creative, be open minded, but remember, only make a deal that makes sense.

Become a skilled negotiator, and you will become a successful real estate investor.

Beware of buying houses that are hard to sell.

# Chapter 15

## Assigning the Contract

An informed investor is in a great position to assign a contract when the information is accurate and well prepared. When putting together your package to present to a prospective investor you will need the following:

- s. A signed contract
- t. Comparable sold properties to support your market value
- u. A written contractor's estimate
- v. Property information form (size, taxes, etc.)

After you have this information together in a folder, it is now time to contact prospective investors. The best way to contact investors is to network. Local real estate clubs are great for this. Start to collect business cards. You may also advertise in your local newspaper, or websites such as Craig's list. Some creative real estate investors put signs on main roads advertising a particular property. You can also distribute flyers. Remember, after each transaction you will build on your investor list.

*How much should an assignment amount be? That depends on the property, the purchase price, and how much profit there is available. It can range anywhere from $1,000 - $20,000 and more. Most of your assignments will probably be from $2,000 – 10,000, averaging about $5,000 an assignment. If you do just one transaction a month, this is not a bad part time income.*

When you meet with your investor, explain how you are assigning this contract. Let them know that time is of the essence and you are speaking with other investors also. Once they have a definite interest and intent to purchase the property, they should then be prepared to put up earnest money. Get in touch with an attorney or title company and submit a copy of the contract and requested information. Inform the attorney or title company that this contract is being assigned, and this information needs to be entered in the closing papers (HUD 1, RESPA).

Even though you have a written contractor's estimate, the investor should still do his own due diligence, including, but not limited to: estimate for repairs, termite and pest inspection, market value, property taxes, etc.

When assigning a contract, don't take anything for granted. Choose a good title company or attorney for the closing. Keep in touch with all parties. Make sure proper inspections are done within time requirements, and that deposit money is put in escrow.

You are well on your way to becoming a real estate pro. Never give up learning, and never give up.

It is all about the win-win.

The ABC's of real estate – Always Be Closing.

# Chapter 16

## Getting Started Before You Get Started

In certain markets, finding the good deals is the easy part. The key to making money in this business is to find the ready, willing, and able investor, or buyer to assign your contract to. You can certainly keep the keepers. There will probably be more deals out there than you can or would want to buy, fix, and personally keep. That is why you want to have a list of investors that you can assign your deals to. Even before you have a contract under contract, you can start to find other investors. Have business cards made, and give them out. Let people know what you do. Attend any type of networking function, and meet people.

The more investors you have, the simpler and quicker you will be able to assign your contracts. Especially with today's computerized technology, it is not unusual to have a list hundreds of investors.

Collect phone numbers, and email addresses. When you have a property tied up, you can send an email to your list of investors, and within hours you may have several people showing an interest. There are a lot of would be real estate investors out there. Some may not be as savvy as you, but only deal with investors who are prequalified for a loan. If someone says they will be paying all cash, it may not be there own. Ask for proof, whether it be in the form of a letter or a bank statement. You certainly don't want to find out at the last minute that the money is not there.

   Before getting started, you should get prequalified for a loan. Even if you don't intend on personally purchasing the property, and will be assigning the contract, having a prequalification letter will help. Many times the seller, whether it is the bank or someone else, will require this. If you are not in a position to qualify for a loan at this time, take on a partner. Many partners work well together in real estate. Your partner may possess skills that you lack, and help advance your success much further along, than if you were to go it solo. Just be careful who you partner up with. You may choose a partner on a deal by deal basis, or someone to be part of the business with you.

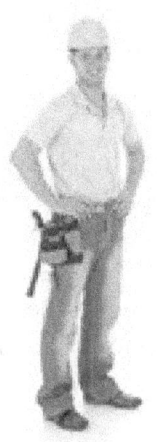

# Chapter 17

## Choosing a Contractor

      Many people have been burned by fly-by-night contractors, or contractors who only have their own best interests at heart. Choose a contractor very carefully. He will be part of your success team. Ask if he is licensed, and what type of licenses does he hold? Does he do plumbing and electric as well as carpentry and roofing? He may not do all of these things, but still be a good person to work with. You just need to know these things up front. A contractor who comes with a recommendation is good. A contractor who comes with many recommendations is better. This is still no guarantee though that this person will not disappoint you down the road.

      Ask for the contractor's business card. Does it have his address on there? Does it have a license number? Does anything look suspicious? Does he have insurance? Does he work alone or with a crew or helper? Does he carry workers comp.? Does he ask for all of the money up front, in cash? What kind of vehicle does he drive? How long has he been in business for? What hours can he be reached at? Does he work weekends?

If he suggests skipping the permitting process, or wants you to apply for it, this is a red flag. Be careful of people who go knocking door to door looking for business. On the surface, they seem like ambitious people who will work hard and give you a real good deal. Maybe, but they may also not be local, not licensed, and not to be found if something goes wrong. Do your homework on everyone you will do business with.

Check around for prices. Call three different contractors, and you will get three different estimates. The lowest price is not always the best one, but he may be. The highest price person may be the best person, or he may not be. Do they charge to give an estimate, and if so, how much? Is this person on the ball and responsible? Do they clean up after a job? Do they have any restrictions? Do they put down carpet, as well as paint, and repair plumbing? Are they afraid of certain jobs, like the kind you will likely come across? Some contractors don't care much for fixer uppers, and houses in very poor condition.

Beware of the contractor you choose.

There are many good contractors, be sure to do your homework.

A good contractor is part of your success team.

You will be very successful if you continue to invest in real estate.

# Chapter 18

## Purchasing to Hold as a Rental

There are numerous ways to make money as a real estate investor. You can buy it and flip it, or you can buy, fix it, and flip it. You can assign the contract, or you can hold it as a long term rental, or buy it and sell it as a lease-purchase. These are a few options to consider. You may decide from the outset what your game plan is, or you may focus on finding as many good deals as you can, and then decide what to do from there. A good game plan is to assign most properties, and keep the good ones for long term rentals. Building a portfolio of rental properties is a great way to build wealth. Even with the ups and downs of the real estate market, over the long term, real estate will appreciate. You can also get some tax write-offs. When you are making the big bucks from assigning contracts, you will appreciate these write-offs.

When you qualify a property to hold onto as a rental, you may look at it a little differently. You will certainly qualify it differently. When you own and manage your own property, you will have a better understanding of what other investors are looking for. You can also purchase a property that may be a terrific deal, but just does not have investors banging down your door at the moment. Now your plan may be to purchase the property, hold onto it as a rental, maybe do some repairs, and raise the rents, and then sell it for a nice profit. Being in the rental business has its pros and cons. The number one rule in real estate applies here, more than ever. <u>Location, location, location.</u> Here is a list of some of the pros and cons to consider:

## Pros:

- Appreciation – Although real estate goes through its cycles, generally, the longer you hold onto a property, the more it will appreciate. This is a big reason why real estate investors become wealthy.

- Cash flow – You want cash flow, you need cash flow, and you will love cash flow. As time goes on, you can raise rents, which will increase your cash flow.

- Equity build-up – When you pay your mortgage each month, a part of that goes toward the principal. As you amortize your loan, initially you will pay mostly interest, and a small amount toward principal. Each month you will start to pay more toward principal, and a little less toward interest. As you pay toward the principal, you are building equity. You can also gain equity as the property appreciates.

- Tax write offs – No one enjoys paying taxes. Being able to write-off repairs and different expenses helps to make real estate the great wealth builder it could be. Even though a property increases in value, you are able to depreciate it on paper, and write this amount off. As you start to make substantial profits in real estate, you will be looking for these write-offs.

- Great retirement plan – When you look at all of the wealth building benefits associated with real estate, it just makes for a great retirement plan. Real estate is truly the IDEAL investment.

Income
Depreciation
Equity build-up
Appreciation
Leverage

# Cons:

- Management – Managing a property is work. Managing a property with a problem tenant is aggravating work. There are other factors also, dealing with repairs, paying bills, maintenance. Etc.

- Dealing with tenants – Some people are a pleasure to work with. Other people only care about themselves, and these types of people you want to stay far away from.

- Dealing with repairs - If you are handy, this may not be a big deal. Try to do the small things by yourself. Repairs can add up and be costly. Try to have the tenant be responsible for most repairs and maintenance.

- Over time, the property may require major upgrades, such as a new roof or air conditioning unit – do your homework, but always be prepared for the unexpected.

- Vacancy issues

- Possible negative cash flow

- Possible being caught in a depreciating market ( it can happen ).

Managing real estate is not for everyone, while others are fine with it. If there is anything about real estate investing you are not comfortable with, but still wish to be involved, you may consider working with a partner. Use caution when choosing a partner. Working with the right partner can make your investing a wonderful experience. Working with the wrong partner is not something to be desired.

As always, look for properties that make sense as an investment. Don't buy just to buy. You may feel like Mr. Big Shot driving through a neighborhood, pointing out the properties that you own. If they are all making money, then you are Mr. Big Shot. If they are not all making money, then you are a real estate investor who wishes he did things differently.

<u>It is better to own two profitable investment properties, than to own ten properties, and only four are profitable.</u>

Time is money, and every time you purchase a property, it is an investment of your time and money. Money can be lost, and made back again eventually. Time can be lost, and it is lost forever. We certainly have more time in our lives, but as time goes on, we have less of it to look forward to. Purchase only properties that make good economical sense. Ask yourself if this is a neighborhood you would want to spend a lot of time in. If you purchase a property in this neighborhood, you may have to spend a lot of time there.

Would you purchase a property with a break even cash flow? Sometimes it makes sense to. If it is in a sound neighborhood, with potential to increase rents, you may consider it. Some properties may have a terrific cash flow, but you still would not want to purchase them. When you are buying a house, you are also buying the neighborhood. As you build your portfolio, choose very carefully. Good deals are like buses; if one passes you by, another one will come along. Just don't get on the wrong one that will take you into the wrong neighborhood.

Purchasing in a good location is of course important, but that is only part of the equation of having an investment that will allow you to sleep well at night. At this stage of the game, you know how to determine market value and repair costs. When this information is accurate, you are in a good position to purchase at the right price that will be profitable. You can have the best property in the best location, but the wrong tenant can make your investment a nightmare. This can not be overstated enough. Most people, when they first come to look at a rental will show their best side. Sometimes the nicest people can turn into the worst.

When showing a property, have the applicant fill out an application. Get their names, current address, and phone number of current landlord, social security number, and date of birth, employer, and employer's phone number. This will be the minimum information you will need. Try to get references, and a credit report. Let them know the rules up front very clearly. If you do not allow pets on your property, tell them, in a nice way, more than once. Don't be surprised though, if you tell them this, and one day you stop by and there is a dog there. They will say they are watching it for someone else. This does happen.

When advertising for a prospective tenant, use multiple sources to attract someone. You can post a sign in front of the house. You can also advertise in the paper, or on websites. Also network to get the word out. Price your rental competitively. Check what other rentals in the area are going for. You don't have to be the lowest, but you do need to be competitive. You may go for 3-4 weeks without any response, and then have 3-4 showings in one day. When showing a rental, make sure it is clean. Remember, they are looking at more places than just yours.

The best tenants are people who keep the place neat and clean, and who pay on time. Tell them the rules up front. You also want to have a rental agreement or a lease that spells out these rules. Don't let someone make it a habit to pay late. Tell them the rules up front, and make sure they abide by them.

The best properties are the ones that you almost never have to visit. The rent comes in, and you pay the mortgage with a smile each month. If you can build a portfolio with this kind of property, you can look forward to a happy, comfortable retirement. Real estate can be a wonderful investment if managed correctly. If real estate management is not for you, hire a property manager, or bring on a partner.

Investing in real estate part time is a great way to build a portfolio over time. There is certainly a fortune to be made investing in real estate, but that does not mean overnight. Learn as much as you can from each property you look at and inspect, and eventually purchase. You may start out slow, and then pick up speed later on. Never stop learning. Always be on the lookout for that great deal. Decide which ones you wish to keep, and assign the rest.

# Chapter 19

## 21 Mistakes Beginners Make, and Sometimes Pros Too

Here is a list of common mistakes, to be aware of:

1. Being over enthusiastic, buying with emotion, not reason – Especially when first starting out, we are all anxious to make a deal. Even the bad deals could seem like they have a lot of potential. The worse a property looks, the more money to be made, right? Not necessarily. At first, as you learn the real estate business, your stock in trade is your desire, emotion, and enthusiasm. This of course is a good thing, for without it, you will not go far. Exercise caution, ask questions, and learn from those who have been there.

2. Not working with accurate information – Knowing is better than guessing. As you gain more experience, your educated guesses

will become more accurate. There is no substitute for accurate information. Confirm all information before taking a final step.

3. **Paying too much for a property** – This happens, and usually is not realized until it is too late. This is one reason it is important to have accurate information. Having an emotional attachment to the property can cause one to pay more. Real estate has its cycles it goes through, and you may find yourself buying at the wrong time of the cycle.

4. **No cash reserves** – This is common, especially amongst beginners. You can do all of your homework, and have accurate information, and there will still be unexpected expenses that come up. Have a back-up financial plan, just in case.

5. **Being greedy** – In the movie Wall Street, Gordon Gecko is quoted as saying "Greed is good". It is a great movie, but greed is not good. Take the profits when you can, don't hold out for the pie in the sky riches. Sell for a realistic price. Rent for realistic market rents. A reasonable profit is better than no profit.

6. **Purchasing a property that requires too much renovation** – Extensive renovation work does not always equate with a lot of profit. The best investment properties are the ones that require the least renovation work. Expect most of the time to clean or repair carpet, paint interior, and maybe repair or replace some minor plumbing and electrical. Renovating kitchens and baths can add much value to a house; it depends on how big of a project you want to take on.

7. **Underestimating repair cost** – Have a qualified contractor give you a written estimate. Even then, you may come across some surprises after you purchase the property. From the basement to the roof, don't take anything for granted.

8. Buying at the wrong time – The contrarian investor philosophy says to buy when others are selling, and to sell when others are buying. This makes a lot of sense. Most people get caught up in the buying frenzy in an overheated market. Take a good long view of the real estate market going back at least five years, and project five years into the future, and see where you stand now. It just may pay to wait a while.

9. Starting out full time – Many people have dreams of grandeur, and becoming the next real estate mogul. Whoever heard of a part time mogul? Now back to reality. Most real estate fortunes are made by people who work at it on a part-time basis. Keep the day job with the income coming in, you will need it also to obtain loans. When your real estate income exceeds your day job income, then consider going at it full time.

10. Neglecting to have a home inspection – You invest a lot of time and effort into finding a potential investment. This could make or break you. Why would you not want to have a home inspection? This is a must for at least two reasons. First, if the inspection uncovers more than you expected or care to handle, back out of the deal. Secondly, the inspection can help you get a lower purchasing price from the seller. If the inspection shows that the house is in sound condition, and there is a not a basis to ask for a lower price, even better. In either case, it is money well spent.

11. Purchasing in the wrong neighborhood – This goes back to our number one rule, <u>location, location, location.</u> Choose the area you want to own property in, and become an expert in the area. You are not only buying a house, you are buying a neighborhood. In lower-end neighborhoods, you can certainly find some bargains, but they are also harder to rent, with more potential problems, and harder to sell.

12. **Not making enough offers** – There is an old Italian saying "If you throw enough spaghetti on the wall, some of it is going to stick." The more houses you look, at the more you will learn. The more you learn, the more comfortable you will be with submitting offers. If your numbers are accurate, the accepted offers will prove to be good deals. Set your goals. Ten offers a week is certainly better than two offers a month. You can be as successful as you aim to be.

13. **Dealing with unmotivated sellers** - Your time is valuable; determine the motivation of the seller upfront, on the phone if possible. Spend your time wisely, tracking down motivated sellers.

14. **Being an uninformed investor (lack of education)** – There is an old story about a man who had a lot of money, who met a man who had a lot of experience. They decided to go in on a venture together. It did not work out the way it was anticipated. The man with the experience ended up with the man's money, and the man with the money ended up with an experience.
You will learn with experience. Learn as much as you can from other's experience as well. Continue to be an informed investor

15. **Renting to the wrong person** – A good tenant can make your real estate investing a wonderful experience. A bad tenant can make life unpleasant. Do as much background checking as possible. And listen to your intuition. Ask about income, and current employment. Why are they moving? Ask many questions.

16. **Purchasing too far away** – Make your investing convenient. There may be some good reasons for investing further away from home, but there are far too many reasons to invest closer to home.

17. Buying houses that don't cash flow – You need to get a return on your money. You need cash flow for expenses and unforeseen circumstances. If you don't have the cash flow, you will be taking it from your own pocket. Let the house support itself, and more.

18. Purchasing without an exit strategy – You now have the great deal, what do you do with it? In many cases, your end use, and exit strategy for this property will determine how you finance it, and to what extent your renovation work will be. Sometimes you can line up a buyer even before you purchase the property. Have a proper game plan.

19. Taking on a tough first project - The first one, in many respects, is the most important one. It can be a motivating experience or have disastrous effects. The first property will be a learning experience. Expect the unexpected. Save the tough projects for later, if you want to take them on.

20. Not having the right success team – This is something that many people take for granted. You will find that the more experienced and successful real estate investors have a team of people that they can depend on. Your success team should include, but not be limited to: your real estate agent, title company or attorney, contractor, handyman, plumber, electrician, banker, and/or mortgage rep.

21. Not having the proper escape clauses – They all look like good deals up front, and the seller seems like a nice guy. Don't let your guard down. Know what escape clauses you need, and use them. Here are a few:

        Subject to partners approval
        Subject to final inspection
        Subject to financing
        Subject to finding a new Buyer/Assignee

Sometimes, being a real estate investor can be frustrating…

But, hang in there, if you persist, you will succeed, and be successful.

Real estate investing can be very lucrative.

# Remember:

No deal is better than a bad deal.

Success happens when preparation meets opportunity.

There is power in setting goals; write yours down, review them periodically

Success must be continually pursued each day.

*"I believe that the true road to preeminent success in any line is to make yourself master of that line."*
-Andrew Carnegie

*"As a rule, he or she who has the most information will have the greatest success in life."*
- Benjamin Disraeli

*"Self trust is the first secret of success."*
- Ralph Waldo Emerson

*"No man is ever whipped, until he quits ...in his own mind."*   -
Napoleon Hill

*"Nurture your mind with great thoughts, for you will never go any higher than you think."*
- Benjamin Disraeli


*"Employ your time in improving yourself by other men's writings, so that you shall gain easily what others have labored hard for."*
- Socrates

*"The secret of success is constancy of purpose."*
– Benjamin Disraeli

*"We are what we repeatedly do. Excellence, then, is not an act, but a habit."* - Aristotle

*"Follow your heart, and your dreams will come true."* - Anonymous

*"Excellence is not a destination; it is a continuous journey that never ends."*
- Brian Tracy


About the author – Pat Esposito is a long time real estate investor and entrepreneur. He has been involved in real estate investing from residential to commercial, and has been a real estate trainer, agent, consultant, and of course, investor. Pat is an author and also the founder of www.theinformedrealestateinvestor.com

*"Reading is a basic tool in the living of a good life."*
- *Mortimer Adler*

www.ingramcontent.com/pod-product-compliance
Lightning Source LLC
Chambersburg PA
CBHW051725170526
45167CB00002B/806